WAL

the GRE LYNN

CW01662027

Number Fifty Nine in the popular series
of walking guides

Contents

Walked, Written and Drawn by Clive Brown
© Clive Brown 2009 – 2019

Published by Clive Brown
ISBN 978-1-907669-59-0

PLEASE
Take care of the countryside
Your leisure is someone's livelihood

Close gates
Start no fires
Keep away from livestock and animals
Do not stray from marked paths
Take litter home
Do not damage walls, hedgerows or fences
Cross only at stiles or gates
Protect plants, trees and wildlife
Keep dogs on leads
Respect crops, machinery and rural property
Do not contaminate water

Although not essential we recommend good walking boots; during hot weather take something to drink on the way. All walks can easily be negotiated by an averagely fit person. The routes have been walked and surveyed by the author, changes can however occur, please follow any signed diversions. Some paths cross fields which are under cultivation. All distances and times are approximate.

The maps give an accurate portrayal of the area, but scale has however been sacrificed in some cases for the sake of clarity and to fit restrictions of page size.

Walking Close To have taken every care in the research and production of this guide but cannot be held responsible for the safety of anyone using them.

During very wet weather, parts of these walks may become impassable through flooding, check before starting out. Stiles and rights of way can get overgrown during the summer; folding secateurs are a useful addition to a walker's rucksack.

Thanks to Angela for help in production of these booklets

Views or comments? walkingcloseto@yahoo.co.uk

Reproduced from Ordnance Survey Mapping on behalf of The Controller of Her Majesty's Stationery Office. © Crown Copyright License No. 100037980.

For Ted Brown 1930-2007

Walking Close to the Great Ouse near King's Lynn

Known only as Lynn by local people, the town was originally called Bishop's Lynn when it was part of the estate of the Bishop of Norwich. Henry VIII confiscated the property during the reformation and it became King's Lynn. The first mention of the town in history is the building of St Margaret's Church in 1101 but the settlement goes back to pre-Roman times; the name is a corruption of Llyn the Celtic word for lake. By the 14th century King's Lynn was, after London and Bristol, the country's third busiest port. The discovery of the Americas however led to ports on the west coast becoming gradually more important.

The fourth longest river in England, the Great Ouse flows 150 miles from Syresham, near Brackley in Northamptonshire through Buckinghamshire, Bedfordshire, Cambridgeshire and Norfolk to the Wash at King's Lynn. The name Ouse is simply the Celtic word for water; the 'Great' distinguishes it from the several other Ouse rivers in England. The river is navigable all the way to Kempston Mill, south west of Bedford.

The River Nar (walks nos 5 and 6) flows for only 15 miles from Litcham, through Castleacre and Narborough to join the Great Ouse in King's Lynn. The length of the River Babingley (walk no2) is only slightly shorter at 12 miles; from its source close to the B1153 near Congham, the River Cong runs just over two miles to join the Babingley on the other side of the A148.

Castle Rising (walk no 2) was once close enough to the sea to be a thriving port; it is now nearly five miles away. The castle was built in the middle of the 12th century by William d'Albini who had married the widow of Henry I. Between 1331 and 1358 the castle was the nominal prison of Queen Isabella (1295-1358), the widow of Edward II, nicknamed the She-Wolf of France. Isabella had led a revolt in 1327 and with the aid of her lover Roger Mortimer she deposed Edward II and installed her son Edward as king. Edward III began his reign as a minor but in 1330 he took control of the kingdom, executed Mortimer and exiled Isabella to Castle Rising. Her imprisonment was however quite comfortable and she was allowed considerable freedom to travel. Intriguingly she was buried in her wedding dress holding her husband's heart. The castle is now in the care of English Heritage.

We feel that it would be difficult to get lost with the instructions and map in this booklet, but recommend carrying an Ordnance Survey map. The walks are on Explorer Maps nos. 236 and 250; Landranger coverage at a smaller scale is on map no 132 (a small section of walk no 10 is on map no 131). Roads, geographical features and buildings, not on our map but visible from the walk can be easily identified.

1 Leziate Heath

$6^1/_4$ Miles 3 Hours

Use the car park of Bawsey Country park, off the B1145 between King's Lynn and Gayton. No facilities, picnic tables only.

1 Leave the car park by the exit at the top left corner (next to the Danger signpost), keep left at the sandy clearing and pass left of the lake. Continue along the path through the trees, follow the path right, uphill to the Danger Deep Cliffs signpost and turn left on the narrower path through the bushes. Go through the wooden barrier and take the path left at the top of the slope with the wire fence the left, bearing right, down to the road.

2 Turn left along the roadside path, past the gates to Leziate Park and follow the roadside track down to the T-junction with the B1145. Keep ahead past the signpost along the wide sandy track with the fence and Leziate Heath to the left.

3 At the signpost turn right and follow the path upslope between hedges, bear left through a clearing, then right along a farm track. At the road turn left for 30yds to the signpost in the hedge gap on the right, go through and follow the field edge left, parallel with the road.

4 Turn right down the narrow tarmac/gravel farm road and continue direction on the grass track beneath overhanging trees. At the end of the path turn right between the houses back up to the B1145.

5 Cross and keep direction along the footpath ahead between fields, follow the farm road right at the junction and continue direction through the farmyard to the road. Keep ahead along the lane almost opposite left to All Saints Church, go into the churchyard, turn left at the church door and follow the arrowed direction from the gate across the wasteground. Join the more substantial access road over a hump and maintain direction through a hedge gap in the corner. Go left through a hedge gap after 200yds and then right to continue with the hedge on the right down to the road.

6 Turn left, down to the corner and take the hardcore road to the right; after almost exactly a mile, fork right at a junction, past the '40' signs and carry on to the road. Take the roadside path to the right up to the sandy/hardcore road on the left.

7 Follow this access road left for 500yds to a wooden barrier on the right, go through and walk along the sandy track through the trees, bearing left then right. Keep on the track upslope and continue as it descends to the car park.

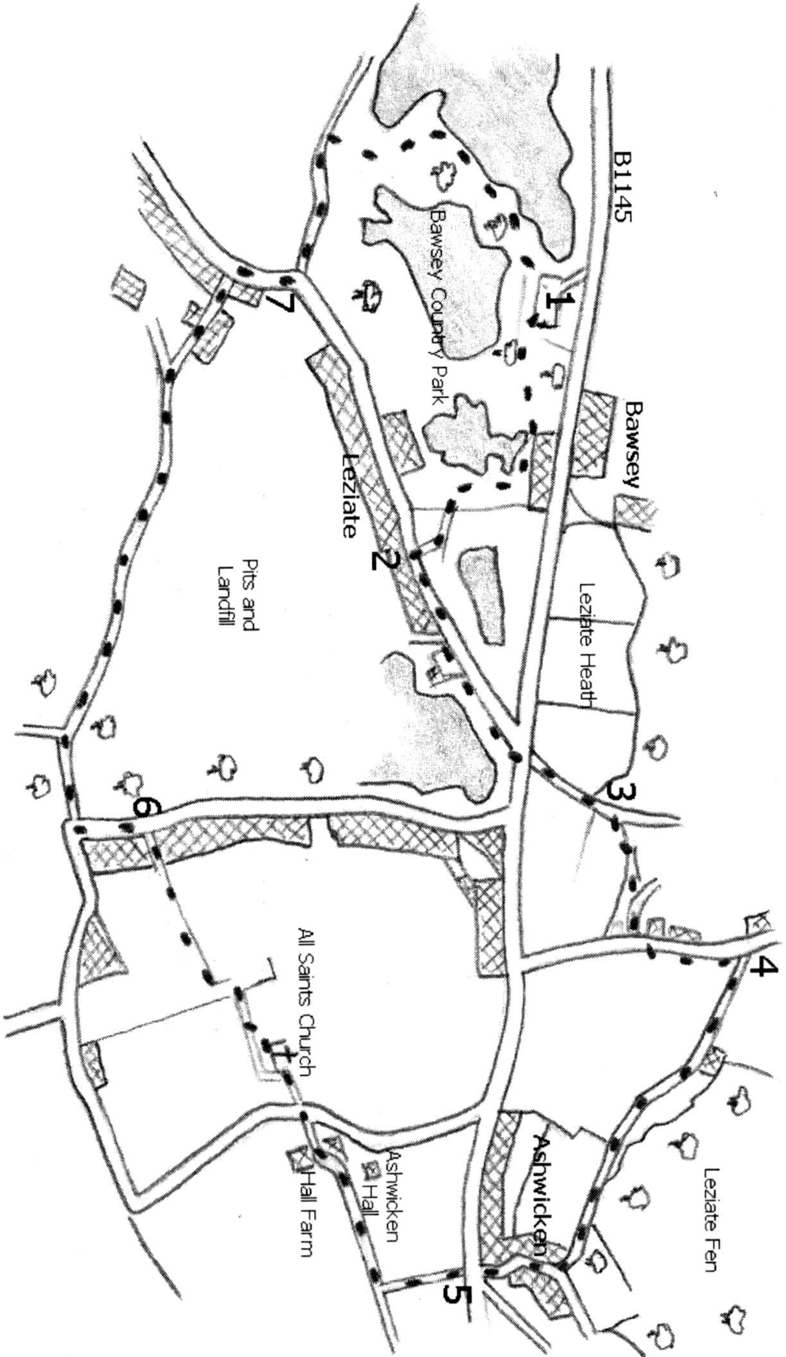
B1145
Bawsey Country Park
1
7
Bawsey
Leziate
2
Pits and Landfill
Leziate Heath
3
6
4
All Saints Church
Ashwicken
Ashwicken Hall
Hall Farm
5
Leziate Fen

2 Onion Corner

$7^1/_4$ Miles $3^1/_4$ Hours

Find a parking space in Castle Rising village. No toilets; pub the 'Black Horse Inn' and tearoom.

1 Start along the old road to the north. Walk up to the wooden kissing gate on the left at the signpost, go through and cross over the cattle grid. Carry on with the wall to the left over the next cattle grid and keep direction along the road between hedges to the junction where the road swings left.

2 Bear right on the sandy hardcore track up to the barn and take the track left along the field edge with the trees and hedge to the right. Bear left and cross over the drive at the signposts and continue on the narrower path through the trees all the way to the road. Turn right, to the '30' signpost.

3 Take the track left through the trees of Ling Common with the houses to the right, follow the track right and left and continue with the houses again to the right. Cross a wooden handrailed footbridge and continue with trees to the right rather than houses. The path leads to a footbridge with a piece of green angle iron sticking out of the ground on the right, as the houses reappear on the right.

4 Turn left this side of the footbridge, with the shallow dyke to the right and walk up to the two sleeper footbridge on the right. Cross and turn immediate left to continue direction with the dyke now left. Continue to the junction close to the road and turn right on the path parallel to the road; take the path to the left and cross the surprisingly busy road to the signpost opposite. **It is very easy to get lost in the trees of Ling Common, if there is a problem, find the sandy parking area on the eastern side of the main road. The path parallel to the road leads south west from the bottom end.**

5 Follow the path through the trees, keep ahead on the hardcore path through the golf course (be careful crossing any fairways), the path bears right and carries on between trees to the A148 road. Cross this busy road carefully and turn left along the grass verge for a third of a mile to the road on the left just before the roundabout at Knights Hill.

6 Take this narrow road left for 600yds to the stile on the right where the road bears right. Step over and walk up the right hand field edge of both fields, go through the gap and cross the busy A149 with great care. Carry on ahead past the signpost, through the hedge gap and up the right hand field edge with the houses to the right. Follow the track right, to the tarmac farm road and turn left past the farm buildings back to the A148.

59:A

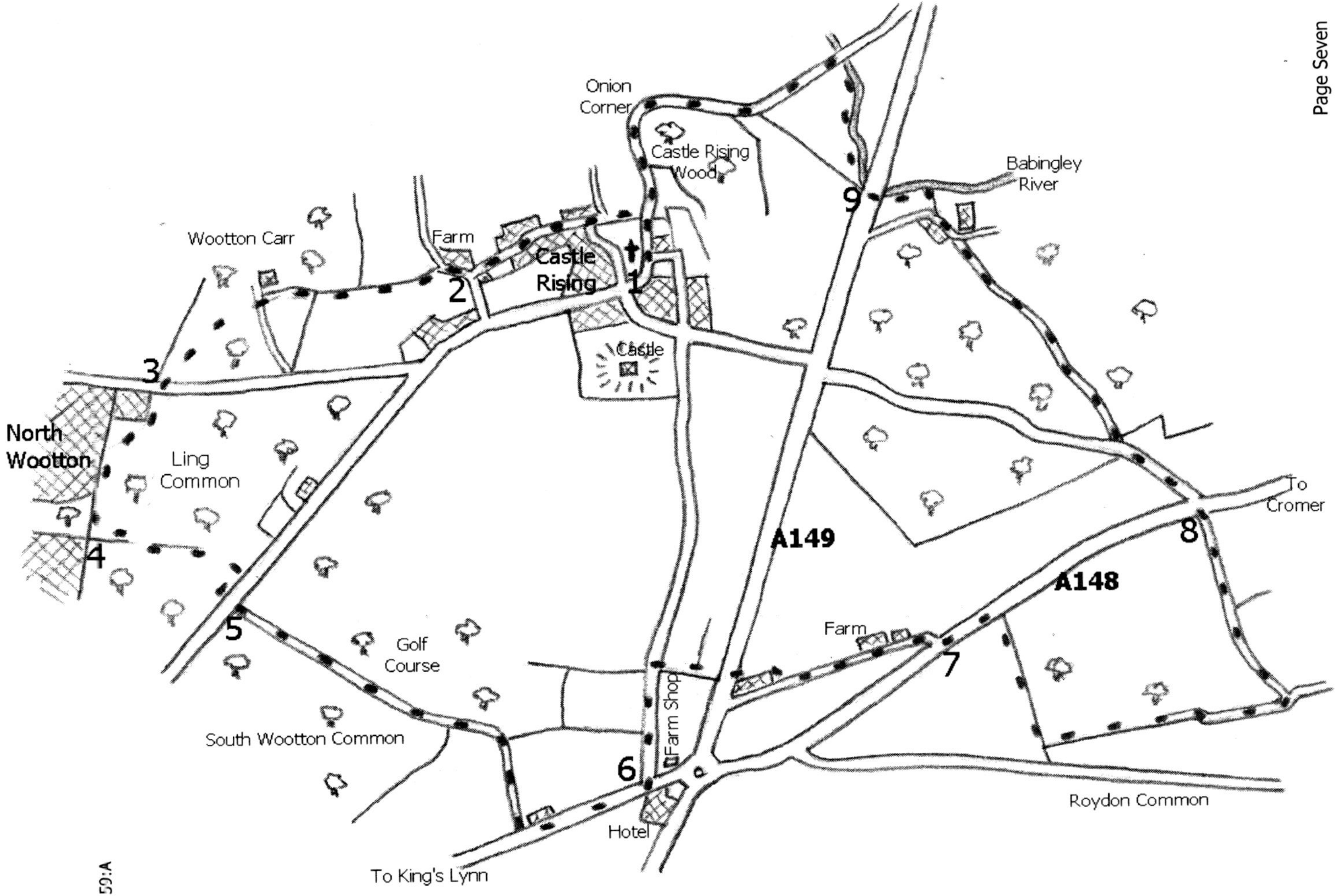
North Wootton
Ling Common
Wootton Carr
Farm
Castle Rising
Onion Corner
Castle Rising Wood
Babingley River
Castle
3
2
1
9
4
5
A149
A148
8
7
6
To Cromer
Farm
Golf Course
South Wootton Common
Farm Shop
Hotel
Roydon Common
To King's Lynn

59:A

Completion of 2 Onion Corner from the previous Page

7 Cross this busy road and turn left along the grass verge to the signpost on the right. (Keeping ahead along the grass verge of the road will lead directly to point **8** and cut a mile and a quarter from the walk total). Turn right, down the left hand field edge with the trees to the left, to the marker post on the left. Take the field edge left with the fence and hedge to the right; partway up the slope follow the track right, through the hedge gap and continue with the hedge now left. Keep on this farm road through the boundary down into the next corner. Turn sharp left past the marker post and follow the field edge back to the A148.

8 Keep direction up the road nearly opposite just into the trees and step over the stile on the right. Follow the path slight left between fences, go past the signpost at the houses and keep ahead to the narrow road. Continue left/straight on to the junction and keep straight on past the signpost on the narrow path between the fence and the hedge. Go over the stile on the left and take the path with Babingley River to the right.

9 Cross back over the A149 past the signpost and bear right along the low embankment with the river still right, carry on to the road. Turn left and follow the road, bearing right at Castle Rising Wood and the long sweep left at Onion Corner. Keep ahead through the gate, back into the village to find your vehicle.

---

3 Middleton Common

6 Miles 3 Hours

Find a parking space in East Winch. Pub the 'Carpenters Arms'. This path will be re-routed at some time in the next few years due to Quarrying, the new route will be well signposted.

1 Start from the church; walk away from the village along Church Lane and bear right at Manor Farm, through the gateposts along the hardcore farm road between grass fields.

2 Continue past the gate at the cottages close to Lower Farm, with the trees, the quarry and the tip to the right. Keep on this track through the bushes and trees to the road at a corner.

3 Turn right, upslope, on this road, past the quarry entrances to the T-junction. Keep direction along the hardcore bridleway between hedges. Keep direction on the stony track to the right of mill Farm, all the way to the A47.

4 Cross this busy road carefully and follow the track ahead bearing left at the end to the road at a corner. Carry on right/ahead along the road into Tower End. Turn right into Tower Lane, past the houses, (*Middleton Towers is behind to the left*) and continue to the corner.

5 Turn right, on the track winding its way past, then through Ferretshill Plantation. Turn left with the deep pit to the left and walk towards Grandcourt Farm and go past the black barrier. Bear right, follow the road left to the junction and turn right, upslope between hedges to the signpost on the left, opposite the bungalow.

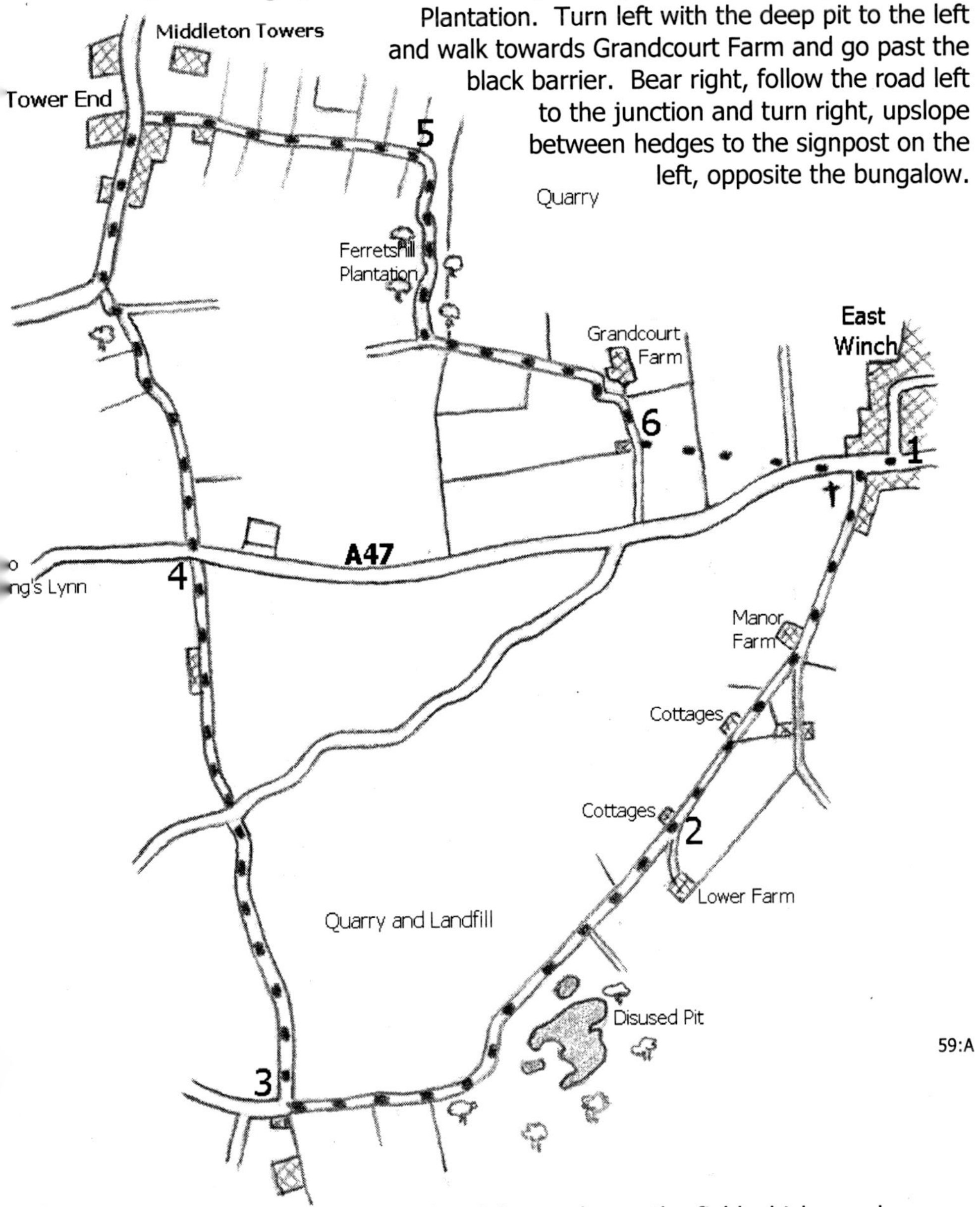

59:A

6 Turn left and take a slight right hand diagonal over the field which may be under cultivation although a path should be well marked within any crop. Continue through the boundary and keep direction to the A47. Turn left, back into East Winch village to find your vehicle.

4 Shouldham Warren

5 Miles 2 Hours

Use the parking area at Shouldham Warren, north of Shouldham village. No facilities; pub the 'King's Arms' in the village.

1 Start along the track to the north, past the information board bearing slight right to a clearing. Bear left back down the slope and keep on this track over a crossroads of tracks and a footbridge.

2 Follow the farm track ahead between fields to the T-junction and take the road left to Wormegay village.

3 Join the road left ahead, in the village centre and follow this road out of the village all the way to Craven Lane.

4 Turn left down this narrow road for two thirds of a mile to the marker post and turn left along the edge of the trees. Continue over the boardwalk and keep direction to a marker post.

5 Bear right and take the narrower, unmarked path moving away from the wide forest road. At the marker post bear left on a wider stony/grass forest road.

6 As this road bears left, bear right to a marker post and follow the field edge left with the trees to the left. Keep ahead at the corner to the marker post, (ignore the arrow pointing straight on!) and turn left along the wider track.

7 Cross the wide and deep Sandy Drain and turn immediate right. Walk along this path with the Drain to the right and the trees to the left all the way back to the car park and your vehicle.

The iconic South Gate at the start of London Road in King's Lynn, dates from the 14th Century. It is actually constructed from bricks and mortar, making it one of the earliest buildings to be built this way. The stone finish is a facing added in 1520, making it also one of the first examples of stone cladding in this country. The unknown but far-sighted architect made the gateway big enough to enable the passage of double decker buses and juggernaut articulated lorries, so it is still in use by traffic entering the town. The out of town route bypassing the gate was opened at the end of the 19th century.

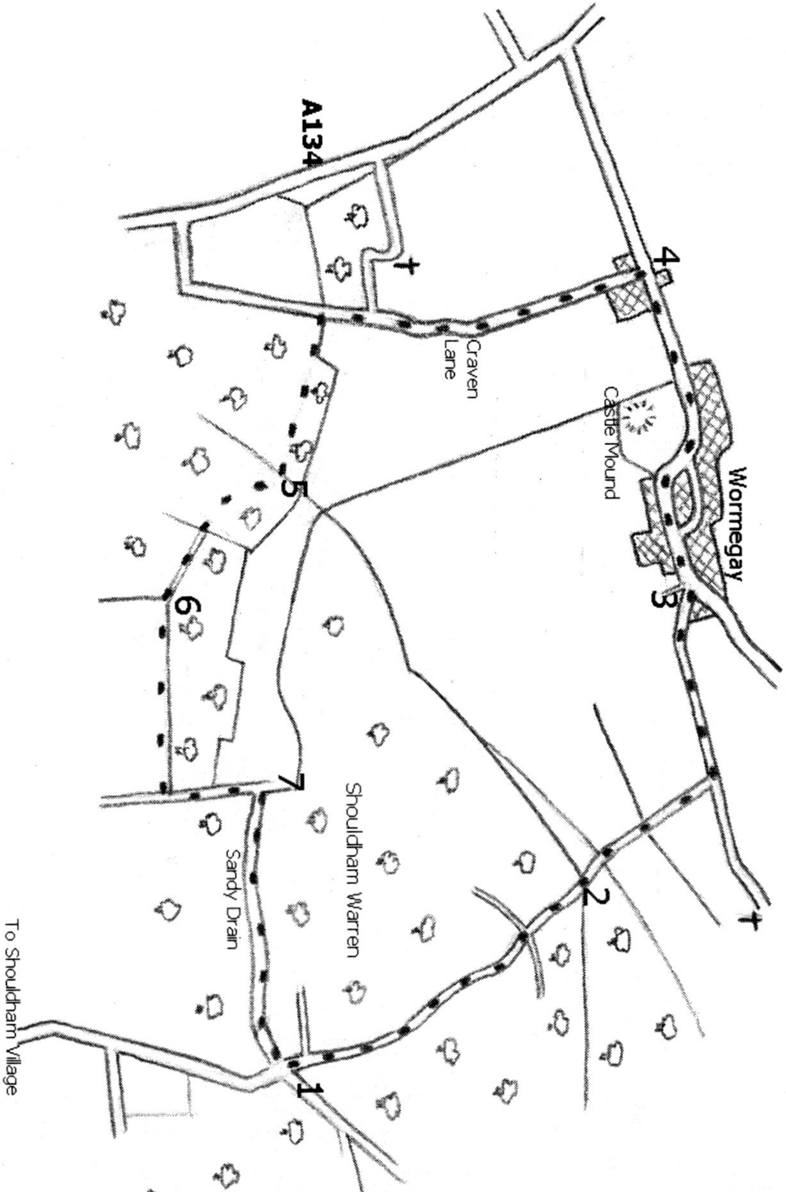

A134
4
Craven
Lane
Castle Mound
Wormegay
3
5
6
7
2
Shouldham Warren
Sandy Drain
1
To Shouldham Village

59:A

Keep direction with the fence to the right, down to the river.

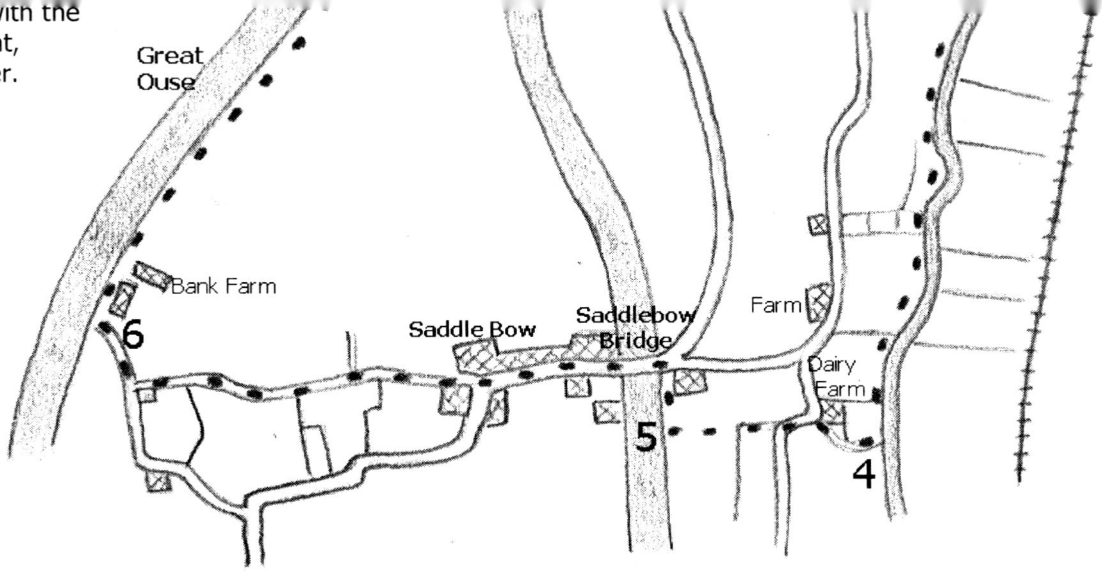

5 Take the path right, along the riverbank to the road and turn left, across Saddlebow Bridge. Carry on up the roadside path; as the road swings left continue straight on along the bridleway with the dyke to the left. Keep direction on this wide hardcore farm track all the way to the road and turn right. Follow the road past the houses and go through the gate.

6 Bear right, up to the top of the embankment and follow the path with the Great Ouse to the left. Bear right along the path through Tail Sluice and turn left, past the green gates back to the river.

7 Carry on with the river again left, back under the A47 and keep ahead over the road at the Free Bridge. Continue direction between the river and the houses, back across the bridge over the River Nar and on to the car park and your vehicle.

5 Saddlebow Bridge

$7^3/_4$ Miles $3^3/_4$ Hours

Use the car park at Boal Street in King's Lynn, pay and display; toilets and all other facilities close by.

1 Start from the rear left of the car park, through the overspill area and past Whitefriar's Gate. Bear right with the embankment to the right, over the bridge at the confluence of the River Nar with the Great Ouse, take the path left, next to the Nar and follow it to the bridge.

2 Turn left and immediate right, along the path with the river now right. Continue with the road left and then between Central Park and the river to the A47.

3 Go under and carry on past the old railway bridges to the farm track, cross the river to the right over the bridge with the round metal railings. Follow this path with the river to the left, for a mile and a quarter, all the way to the marker post close to Dairy Farm.

4 Turn right, along the farm track passing left of the farm buildings, bearing right to the road corner in front of the farm. Turn left to where the road swings left and continue straight on along the wide farm track and up the slope of the embankment.

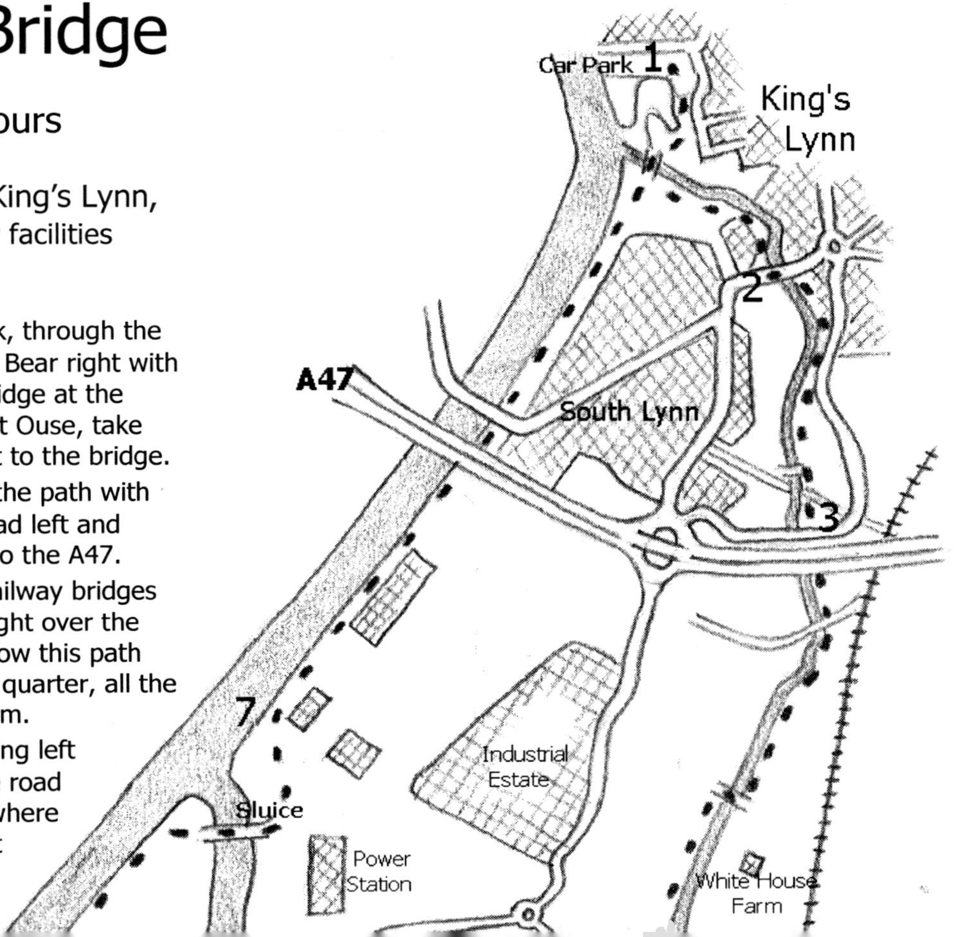

6 Marham Fen

$5\frac{1}{4}$ Miles

$2\frac{1}{2}$ Hours

Find a parking space in Narborough; no toilets, shop/post office.

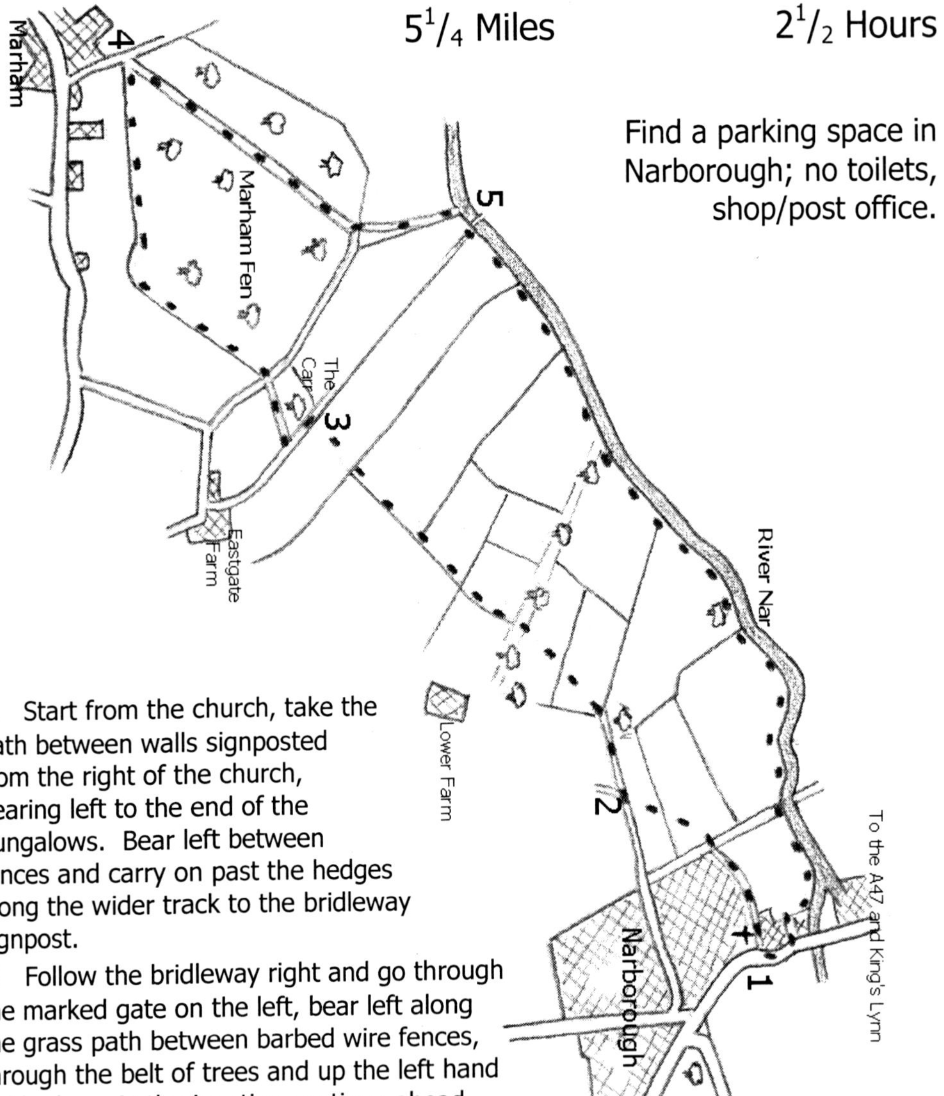

1 Start from the church, take the path between walls signposted from the right of the church, bearing left to the end of the bungalows. Bear left between fences and carry on past the hedges along the wider track to the bridleway signpost.

2 Follow the bridleway right and go through the marked gate on the left, bear left along the grass path between barbed wire fences, through the belt of trees and up the left hand field edge. At the junction continue ahead slight right and keep direction along the field edge with the hedge and the dyke to the left; cross the footbridge and carry on to the farm road at the trees.

3 Turn left and almost immediate right, through the trees on the edge of The Carr to another farm road. Keep ahead, slight left along the wide track at the edge of Marham Fen, bearing right to the metal gate at the interlocking wire fence.

4 Turn sharp right on the wide track through the trees, go past the metal barrier at the end and continue along the hardcore road to the River Nar.

5 Follow the path right with the Nar to the left up to the edge of Narborough. Take the path right between the bungalows and through River Close to the main road, turn right, back to the church.

---

7 Soigné Wood

$6^1/_2$ Miles 3 Hours

Find a parking space in Gayton Thorpe, south east of Gayton which is on the B1145. No facilities, there is often room near the church.

1 Fork right, along the wide track away from the church, past the black barn and the cottage. Carry on along this track all the way to the road.

2 Turn sharp left, up the field edge with the hedge to the right. Follow the path right and left, back to the original direction and keep on the path as it swings right, through a hedge gap and continues with the hedge now left. Keep ahead through the wide gap in the belt of trees, along the path between fields to the path at the edge of Soigné Wood.

3 Take the track right, bearing left along the edge of the trees into the corner. Turn right up the path with the hedge to the right, at the corner of the trees turn left on the wide farm road for 650yds to the marker post.

4 Turn left up the slope with the hedge to the right and continue along the tarmac road between hedges for just over three quarters of a mile to the crossroads. Turn left, past a low marker post and keep ahead into the corner. At this marker post, turn right past the ruins of the old barn to the lowest point.

5 Take the grass path to the left between fields, through the trees and carry on to the junction of tracks. Bear right with the barn to the right, along the hardcore byway between hedges all the way back to Gayton Thorpe to find your vehicle.

The map for 7 Soigné Wood is on the next Page (Sixteen)

7 Soigné Wood Map

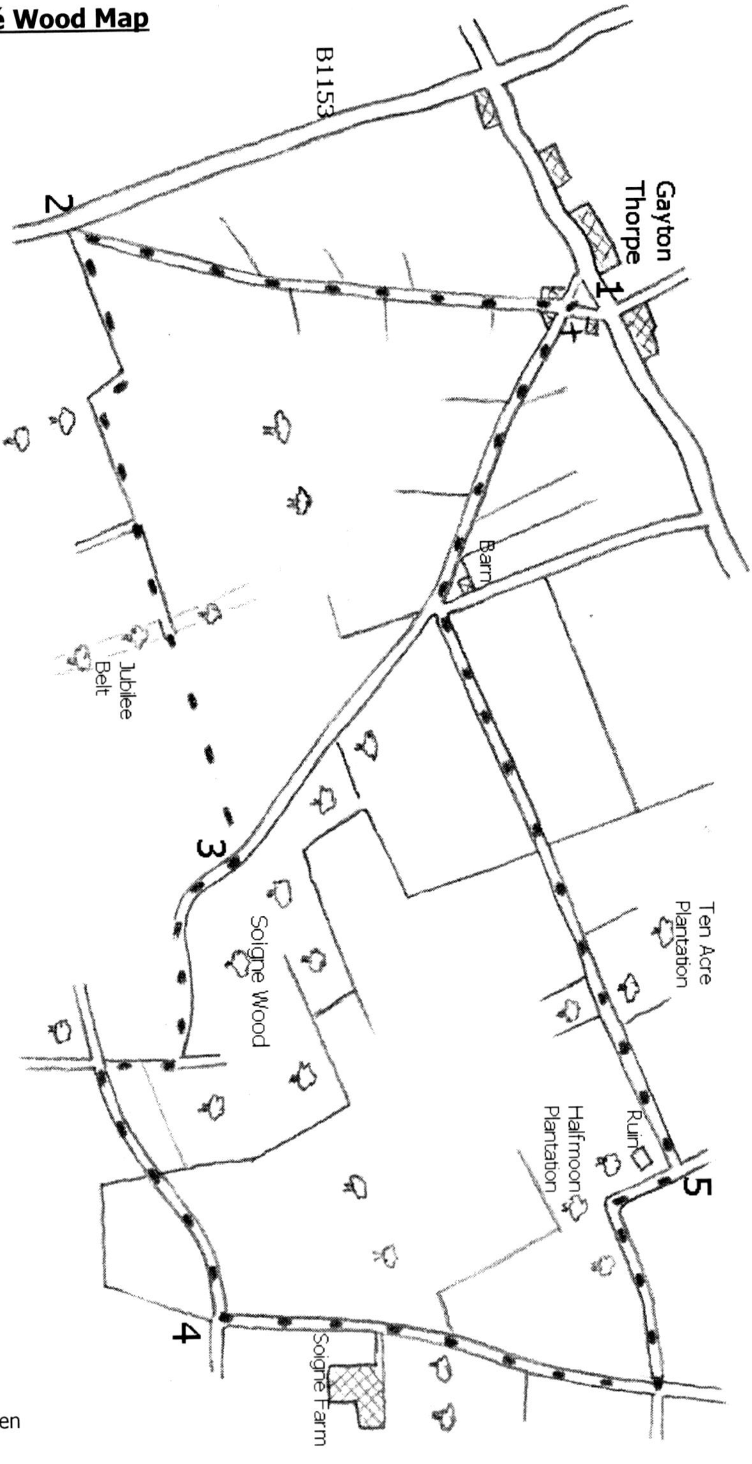

8 Soigné Triangle

$3^1/_2$ Miles $1^1/_4$ Hours

Find a parking space in Gayton Thorpe, south east of Gayton which is on the B1145. No facilities, there is often room near the church.

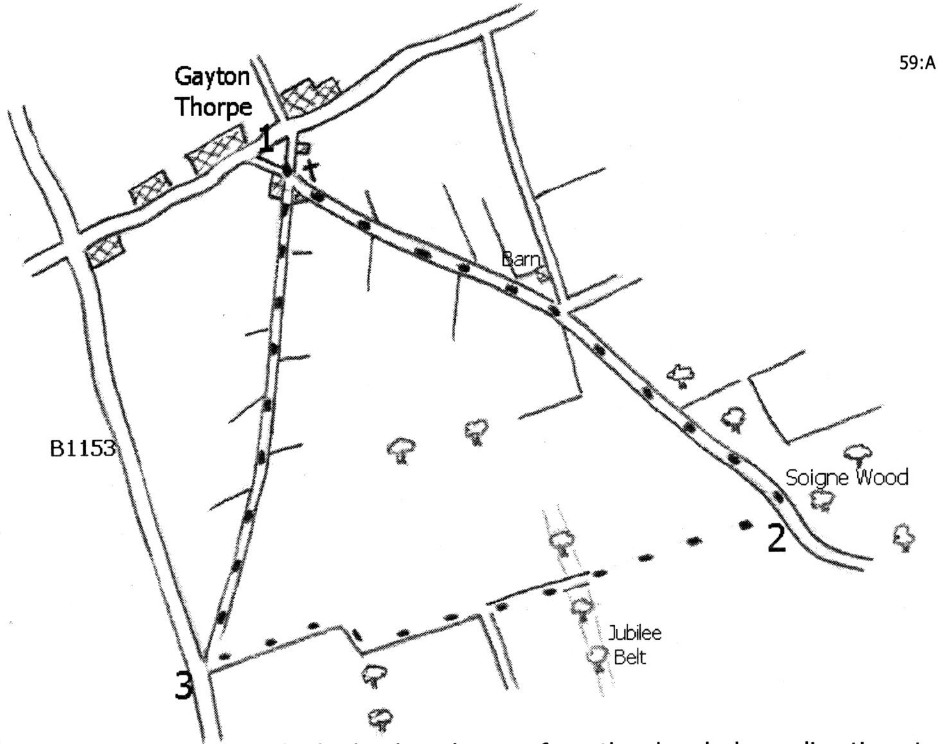

1 Fork left, along the wide, hedged track away from the church, keep direction at the junction by the barn and carry on uphill with Soigné Wood to the left to the marker post on the left near the summit (a gap in the trees leads off to the left).

2 Take the grass track to the right, between fields and continue with the hedge to the right. Bear right, through the hedge gap and maintain direction with the hedge now left, up to the corner. Turn right and then almost immediate left; follow this field edge to the road.

3 Turn sharp right along the path between fields and carry on between hedges, past the silos to the junction at the green in Gayton Thorpe, to find your vehicle.

9 Little Massingham Park

$4\frac{1}{2}$ Miles 2 Hours

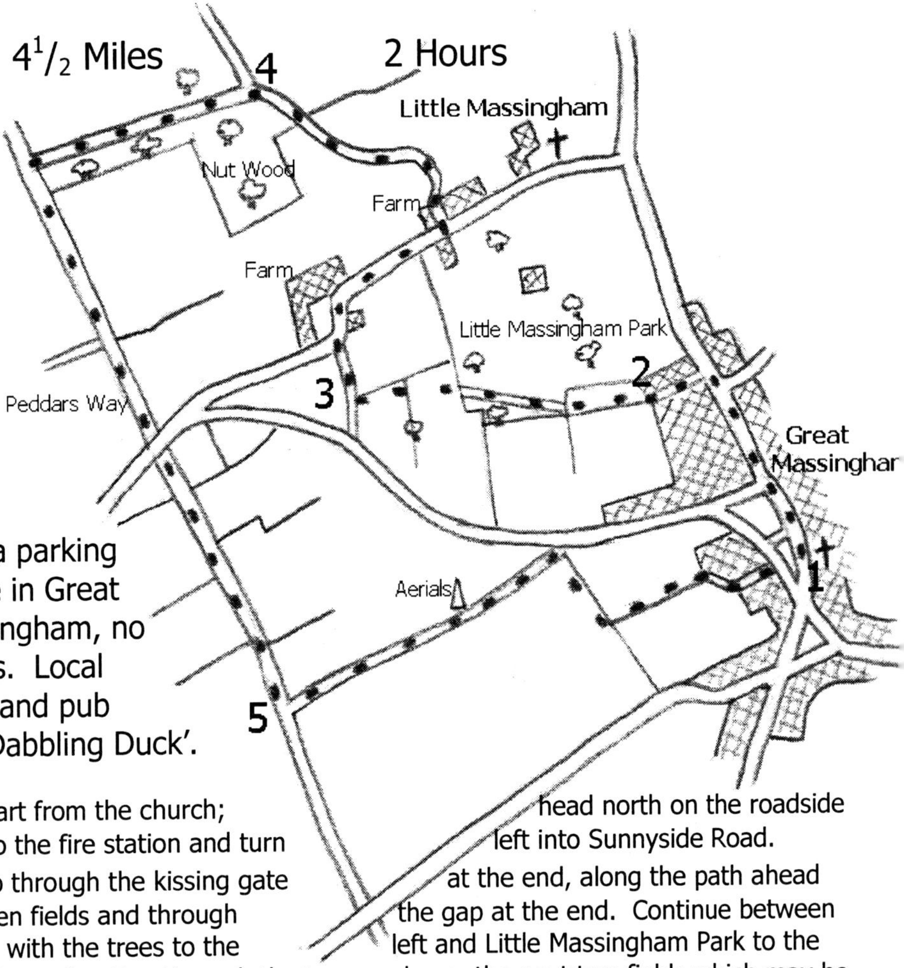

Find a parking space in Great Massingham, no toilets. Local shop and pub the 'Dabbling Duck'.

1 Start from the church; head north on the roadside path to the fire station and turn left into Sunnyside Road.

2 Go through the kissing gate at the end, along the path ahead between fields and through the gap at the end. Continue between fences with the trees to the left and Little Massingham Park to the right, keep direction through the trees and over the next two fields which may be under cultivation although a path should be well marked.

3 Turn right along the path through the trees to the road and turn right, around the double bend to the signpost on the left at Middle Farm. Follow this flinty farm road to the left as it winds its way to the junction at the far corner of Nut Wood.

4 Bear left, with the trees of the wood to the left, to the crossroads of tracks at Peddars Way. Turn left past the inscribed stone on the left and carry on down to the road, cross and continue for a third of a mile to the signposted crossroads.

5 Turn left, past the aerials and the water tank, almost to the road. At the signpost, turn right along the path between fields to the marker post at the boundary. Turn left with the hedge to the right past a low marker post and a brick garage; bear right and left between hedges and keep ahead to the green and Great Massingham Church.

10 Eau Brink

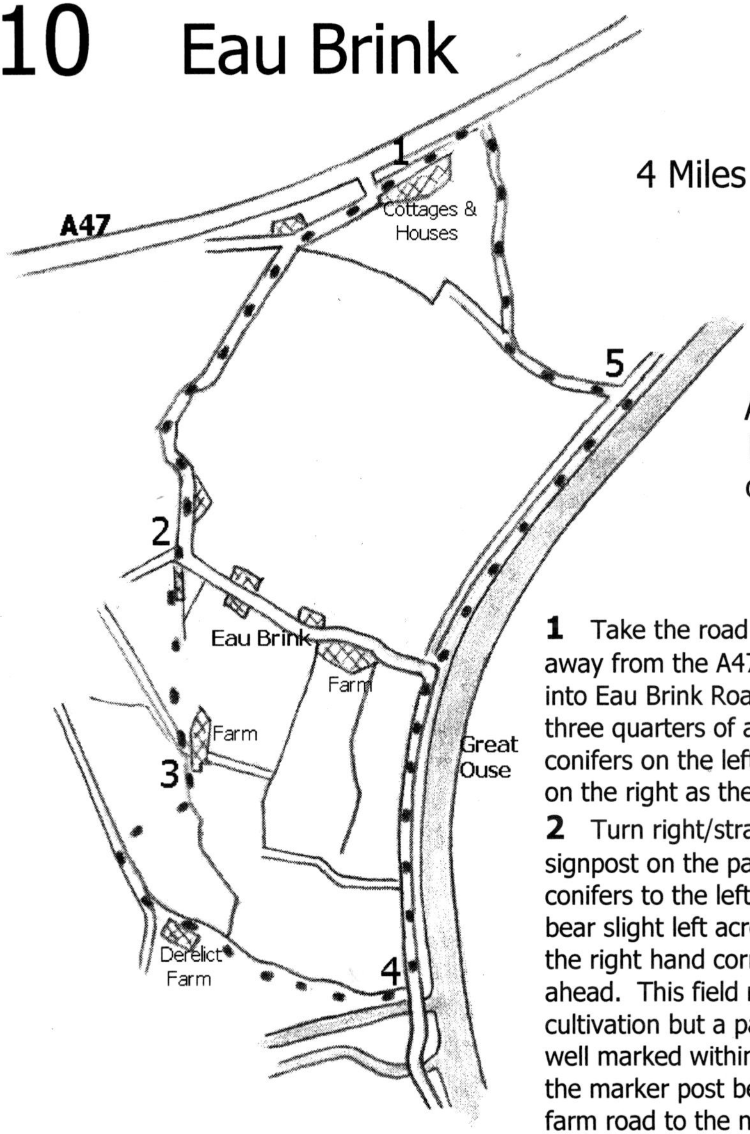

4 Miles 2 Hours

Park in the old section of A47 at Pullover Road, on the A47, one and a half miles west of the A17/A47 junction. No facilities.

1 Take the road west moving away from the A47 and bear right into Eau Brink Road. Carry on for three quarters of a mile, past the conifers on the left to the signpost on the right as the road swings left.

2 Turn right/straight on at the signpost on the path with the conifers to the left. At the corner, bear slight left across the field to the right hand corner of the barn ahead. This field may be under cultivation but a path should be well marked within any crop. At the marker post bear left along the farm road to the next marker post.

3 Go past the concrete standing area with the barn to the left and turn right over the field (a track should be visible) to the wide gap in the hedge at the signpost. Go through and turn left along the stony farm road, as this road bears right at the trees, go straight on along the grassy path through the trees with the dyke still left.

Completed on the next Page (Twenty)

Completion of 10 Eau Brink from the previous Page

Keep on this wide track between the dyke and the field, leading eventually under the wires, through a hedged path to the road.

4 Turn left along the road, (there is a path parallel to the river accessible from the bridge on the right, but it is not a right of way). Keep direction as the road turns left, with the embankment to the right. Step over the stile ahead and bear right, up the incline. Follow the top of the embankment for two thirds of a mile.

5 Turn left and go over the stile at the signpost, take the track bearing right with the dyke to the left. At the second junction of tracks bear right, along to the A47. Turn left along the grass verge of this busy road (or cross and use the roadside path) back to Pullover Road and your vehicle.

11 Crimea Plantation

6 Miles 3 Hours

Park in the long lay-by on the A148 west of Hillington. Spar shop at the garage and pub 'The ffolkes Arms' on the main road.

1 Leave the lay-by to the east, into the village to the junction signposted to Grimston (Station Road). Ascend the steps into the churchyard and follow the path parallel to the road to the bridleway signpost.

2 Turn left up the bridleway, bear right at the barn and take the hedged track left past the pond to the T-junction at the trees. Take the wide byway right, with the trees to the right, and carry on for nearly a mile and a half, into the trees, passing left of Crimea Plantation.

3 At the staggered crossroads in the middle of the wood by the fenced pond, turn right along this wide road all the way to the B1153. Cross and continue ahead along Low Road to the kissing gate 50yds past the end of the houses.

4 Go through and carry on past the front of the thatched cricket pavilion. Pass through the gap in the fence and bear left to the marker post; turn right over the footbridge and left through the fence gap. Take the path to the right, round the double bend and up to the road at Congham.

5 Turn right, along to Church Hill and turn left on this wide hardcore track past the houses all the way to the junction with the tarmac road and bear left/straight on. Follow this tarmac driveway, passing over the narrow River Cong to the road. Turn right along the old road/lay-by to find your vehicle.

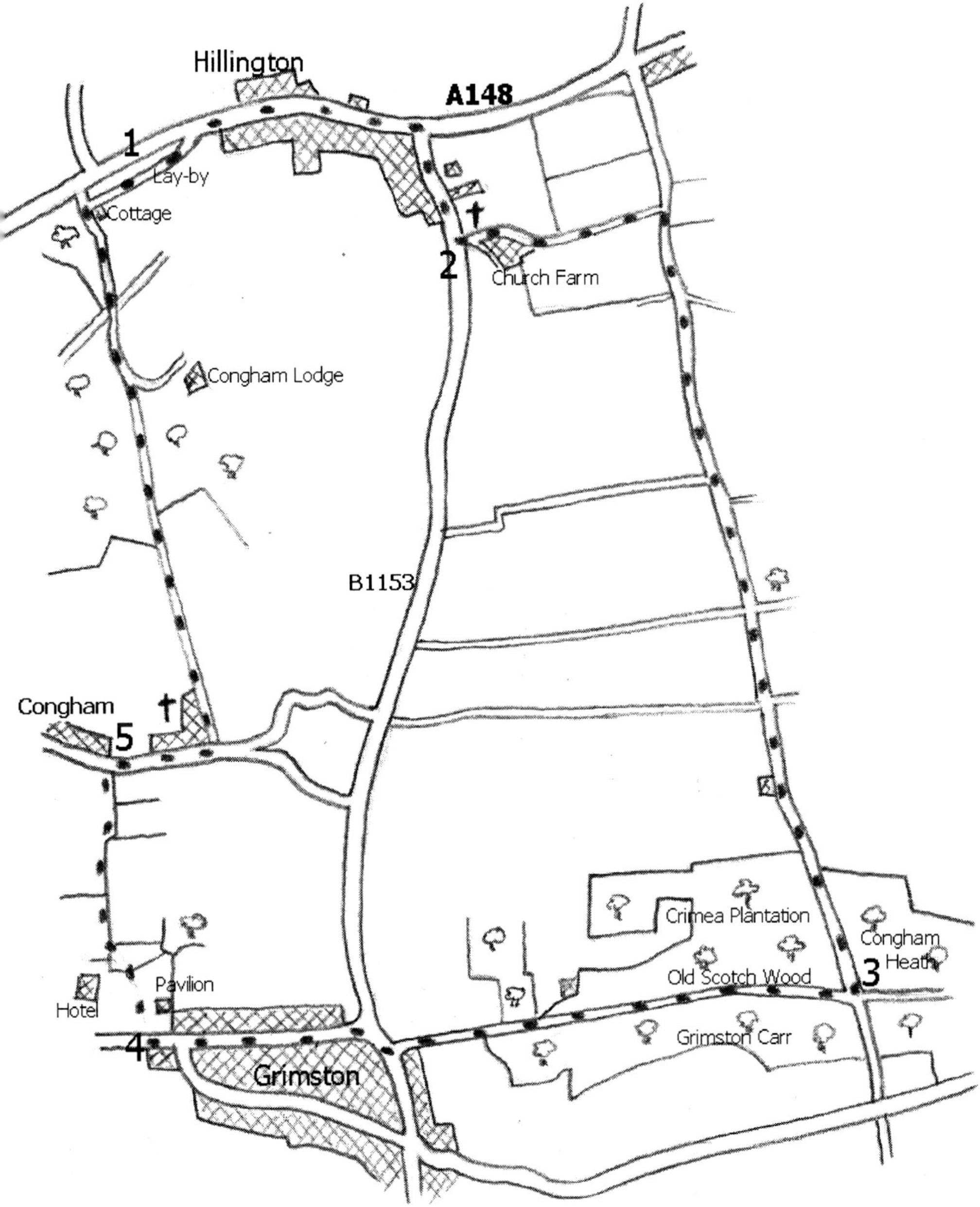
Hillington
A148
1
Lay-by
Cottage
2
Church Farm
Congham Lodge
B1153
Congham
5
Crimea Plantation
Congham
Heath
Old Scotch Wood
3
Pavilion
Hotel
4
Grimston Carr
Grimston

59:A

12 Roydon Common

6 Miles $2^1/_2$ Hours

Use the parking area at the playing field off Chapel Road in Roydon. No toilets; pubs the 'Blacksmiths Arms' and the 'Three Horse Shoes'.

1 Start out of the top of the car park; go through the kissing gate and follow the road to the crossroads. Cross the footbridge opposite and go past the signpost through the bushes, bear left through the tunnel in the undergrowth and join the more substantial track to the left. Carry on past the end of the factory and keep direction through two narrow metal gates.

2 Continue along the road and track ahead between fences then hedges, all the way to the road. Turn left/ahead, down to the junction for Hall Farm; take the entrance road left down to the signpost on the right.

3 Turn right, along this wide farm track; cross to the left at the marker post at the boundary and continue the original direction with the hedge now right. The track swings right again through the hedge and carries on up the narrower path with the hedge again left. At the end, turn left down to the road.

4 Cross carefully and go over the field bearing slight right, to the far boundary. Turn right with the fence and Roydon Common to the left; continue straight on upslope from the corner, through the gap at the top left. Follow the track ahead and join the more substantial track right/ahead, with the fence to the right. Turn left at the end and go through the wide gap.

5 Take the field edge to the right with the hedge to the right and keep direction through boundaries to the farm road above the A149. Turn left down to the narrow tarmac road.

6 Follow this byway to the left, past Warren Farm and bear right at the tall brick piers. Carry on for just over a mile to the hump in the road of the dismantled railway at the white cottage.

7 Turn left through the kissing gate, continue through the next kissing gate and keep direction on the wide path with the deep dyke to the right. Just before the road, turn left into the playing field car park to find your vehicle.

59:A

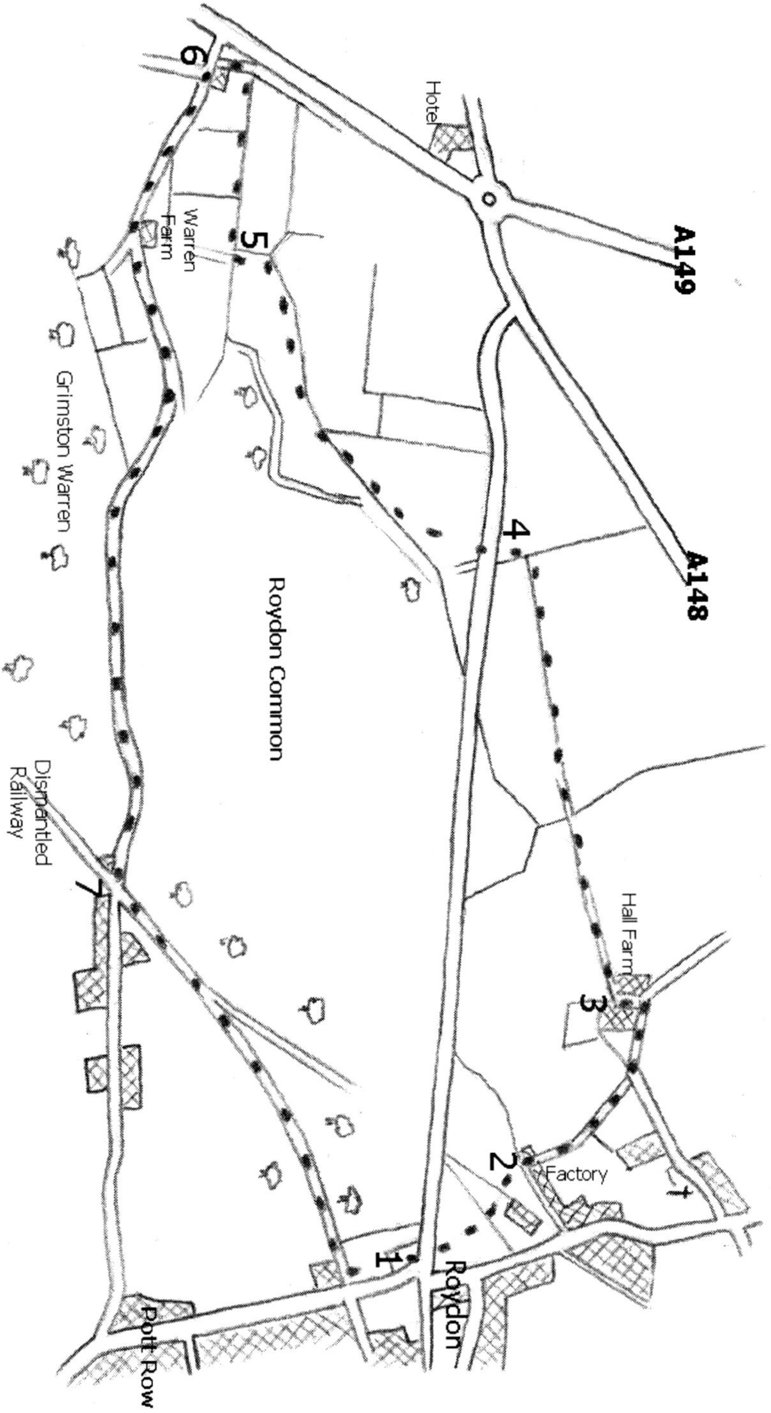
6
Hotel
A149
5
Warren Farm
Grimston Warren
4
A148
Roydon Common
Dismantled Railway
Hall Farm
3
7
2
Factory
1
Roydon
Pott Row

59:A

The 'Walking Close to' Series

South and South West

Salisbury and Stonehenge
The New Forest (North and West)
Romsey and the Test Valley
Cheddar Gorge
Exmouth and East Devon
Corsham and Box (Wiltshire)
The Quantock Hills (West Somerset)
Blandford Forum (Dorset)
Chichester and the South Downs (2019)
Winchester and the South Downs (2019)
The New Forest (South and East)
The East Devon Coast
Glastonbury and the City of Wells
The Avon near Bath
The Avon near Chippenham (Wiltshire)
Shaftesbury (Dorset)
Bradford-on-Avon (Wiltshire)

East Anglia and Lincolnshire

The Nene near Peterborough
Lavenham (Suffolk)
The Nene Valley Railway near Wansford
The Nene near Oundle
The Great North Road near Stilton
Bury St Edmunds
Norfolk Broads (Northern Area)
Southwold and the Suffolk Coast
North West Norfolk (Hunstanton and Wells)
North Norfolk (Cromer and Sheringham)
The Lincolnshire Wolds (North)
The Stour near Sudbury (Suffolk)
Chelmsford
Epping Forest (Essex/North London)
The Colne near Colchester
Thetford Forest (Norfolk/Suffolk)
The Great Ouse in Huntingdonshire
The Torpel Way (Stamford to Peterborough)
Grafham Water (Huntingdonshire)
Dedham Vale (Suffolk/Essex)
The Cam and the Granta near Cambridge
Lincoln
The Welland near Stamford
The Isle of Ely
Norfolk Broads (Southern Area)
Aldeburgh, Snape and Thorpeness
Clare, Cavendish and Haverhill
Bourne and the Deepings
The Lincolnshire Wolds (South)
The Orwell near Ipswich
Stowmarket (Suffolk)
Hertford and the Lee Valley
Newmarket
The Great Ouse near King's Lynn
South Lincolnshire

Midlands

The Nene near Thrapston
The Nene near Wellingborough
The River Ise near Kettering
The Nene near Northampton
Rockingham Forest (Northamptonshire)
Daventry and North West Northamptonshire
Rugby
Stratford-upon-Avon
Rutland Water
Eye Brook near Uppingham
The Soar near Leicester
Lutterworth (Leicestershire)
The Vale of Belvoir (North Leicestershire)
Melton Mowbray
The Welland near Market Harborough
Banbury
South West Herefordshire
The Great Ouse near Bedford
Woburn Abbey (Bedfordshire)
Sherwood Forest
Pitsford Water (Northamptonshire)
The Thames near Oxford
The Trent near Nottingham
The Vale of White Horse
Henley-on-Thames
The River Pang (Reading/Newbury)
The Great Ouse north of Milton Keynes
The Cotswolds near Witney
The Malvern Hills
The Dukeries (Sherwood Forest)
The Severn near Worcester
Woodstock and Blenheim Palace
The Kennet near Newbury

Cumbria

Cartmel and Southern Lakeland